TELL ME WHY, TELL ME HOW

HOW DO MOUNTAINS FORM?

TERRY ALLAN HICKS

mc Marshall Cavendish
Benchmark
New York

Marshall Cavendish Corporation
99 White Plains Road
Tarrytown, NY 10591-5502
www.marshallcavendish.us

Library of Congress Cataloging-in-Publication Data
Hicks, Terry Allan.
How do mountains form? / by Terry Allan Hicks. — 1st ed.
p. cm. — (Tell me why, tell me how)
Includes index.
ISBN 978-0-7614-3992-9
1. Orogeny—Juvenile literature. 2. Mountains—Juvenile literature. I.
Title.

QE621.H55 2009
578.769'9—dc22

2008029434

Photo research by Candlepants Incorporated

Cover Photo: Fernando Bengoechea/Beateworks / Corbis

The photographs in this book are used by permission and through the courtesy of:
Photo Researchers Inc.: Adam Jones, 1; Edward Kinsman, 17; Gary Hincks, 18. *Getty Images*: Christopher Groenhout, 4. *Alamy Images*: Kevin Schafer, 5; All Canada Photos, 6; Brad Mitchell, 8; Buzz Pictures, 11; Ali Kabas, 12; Tom Till, 13; David Noton Photography, 16; Jason Lindsey, 21; Pat Behnke, 26. *Corbis*: DLILLC, 7; 14; Tom Bean, 19; Gary Braasch, 20; Peter Adams/JAI, 22; 24; Phil Schermeister, 25; Craig Tuttle, 27. *Art Life Images*: age fotostock, 10.

Editor: Joy Bean
Publisher: Michelle Bisson
Art Director: Anahid Hamparian
Series Designer: Alex Ferrari

Printed in Malaysia

1 3 5 6 4 2

CONTENTS

These two mountains, part of
Australia's Lord Howe Island, rise out
of the Pacific Ocean.

Mountains Everywhere

Mountains are everywhere on our planet, on every continent and in almost every country. These huge **landforms** cover almost one-quarter of the earth's surface. They are found in tropical rain forests and Antarctic ice fields. They tower above crowded cities and empty deserts. Mountains are even found

Some mountains are covered in snow and ice all year round.

on the ocean floor, sometimes breaking the water's surface to create islands.

Few people live on mountains because conditions there are usually harsh. Mountain air has little oxygen, which makes it difficult for people to breathe. Mountaintops are usually cold because the air there has less water and dust in it than at lower levels. That means the air cannot trap the sun's heat well. Steep mountainsides also make working and traveling difficult. But mountains are still very important. About one-tenth of the world's population lives in mountainous regions. They live mostly on the lower slopes of the mountains, in the **foothills** surrounding them, or in the **valleys** below them.

The higher mountain slopes, where people rarely live, are home to an large variety of wildlife. Giant condors glide through the Andes of South America, and bighorn sheep feed on

The bighorn sheep is taking a rest after grazing on the wild grasses that grow on the mountain slopes.

the wild grasses that grow in the Rockies of the western United States. Even above the **timberline**, the **altitude** above which trees cannot grow, plants including moss, lichen, and delicate flowers survive on steep, rocky mountainsides.

The world's mountains are also important to people and wildlife who live far away from them. The **peaks** of many

Mount Kilimanjaro in Africa has a wide range of climate zones. It has tropical forests at its base and ice at its peak.

Melting snow creates many mountain streams, like this one in the Cascade Range in Washington State.

mountains are covered with snow or ice for at least part of year. Even mountains in very hot places, such as Africa's Mount Kilimanjaro, are topped with snow. When the snow and ice melt, mountain rivers bring life-giving water to at least one-half of the world's population. They also carry soil down into mountain valleys. The soil provides the valleys with some of the richest farmland anywhere.

Mountains are also an important source of **energy**. The force of water from melting snow, when channeled through dams, can be used to create electricity. And the **geothermal energy** produced by certain types of mountains heats homes and powers factories in countries such as Iceland, Japan, and New Zealand.

But what are mountains, exactly, and how are they created?

Mountains can take many forms. Some are sharp and jagged, like these peaks in the Dolomites, in northern Italy.

Is That a Mountain or a Hill?

A mountain is a landform that rises high above the land around it, usually with steep sides and sharp (or sometimes slightly rounded) edges and a clearly defined peak. But when it comes to what makes a mountain a mountain, **geologists**, who are scientists who study the structure of the earth, do not agree on the basics. Some say any landform with an altitude of more than 1,000 feet (305 meters) is a mountain. Others say a mountain must be at least 2,000 feet (610 m) high.

The experts do not even

Some of the world's mountains, like these ones in the desert, are rounded.

11

agree about how to measure a mountain's altitude. The most common way to do this is measure how high its peak is above **sea level**. By this standard, the highest mountain in the world is Mount Everest, at 29,035 feet (8,850 m). Everest is part of the great Himalayan **mountain range**, which extends more than 1,500 miles (2,400 kilometers) across Central Asia. There are 109 mountains in the world that rise more than

Mount Everest, seen here, is usually considered the highest mountain in the world.

24,000 feet (7,317 m) above sea level, and 96 of them are in the Himalayan mountain range.

There are other ways of measuring a mountain. One is to begin measuring at the **base**, the point where the mountain begins to rise from the surrounding area. When this method is used, the highest mountain in the world becomes Mauna Kea, on the Pacific island of Hawaii. Mauna Kea is 13,796 feet (4,200 m) above sea level, but its base is approximately 19,000 feet (5,800 m) below sea level, on the ocean floor. This makes

This is Mauna Kea in Hawaii. Its base lies far below the water, on the ocean floor.

its total height almost 33,000 feet (10,000 m)—even greater than Everest's.

However we measure their height, there is no question that mountains are the highest things on earth. Nothing manmade even comes close. The world's tallest building is a

Olympus Mons (shown here) is a mountain on the planet Mars. It is 375 miles (604 km) wide at the base.

skyscraper being built in Dubai, in the Middle East. When completed, it will be 2,625 feet (800 m) tall. Even so, it would take more than ten such buildings, stacked on top of one another, to equal Mount Everest.

If you want to find the highest mountain known to man, you will need to look beyond our planet. A mountain on Mars, called Olympus Mons, stands 88,580 feet (27,000 m) above the planet's surface. That makes it almost three times as high as Everest is above sea level. It is also more than twice as high as Mauna Kea is above the ocean floor. And we have only begun to explore other planets, so there may be even higher mountains out there, just waiting to be discovered.

A little hut clings to a steep
mountain slope in the Swiss Alps.

Making Mountains

Mountains are the highest structures on the planet, but the forces that create them begin deep beneath the earth's surface. These forces work very slowly, over millions or even billions of years, and they never stop working. This means that new mountains are always being created, and old ones are always being destroyed.

The earth under your feet may feel solid, but in reality, it is always moving. The upper layer of the earth, called the crust, has many different layers of rock, known as **strata**, lying on top of one another. And the crust is made up of huge slabs of rock, sometimes the size of entire continents, called **tectonic plates**, which are constantly pushing and grinding against

Sometimes the layers of a mountain can be seen clearly, as in this picture taken in Canada.

each other. The sudden movement of these plates can cause earthquakes and the great ocean waves known as tsunamis.

Most of the earth's mountains are formed by the movement, fast or slow, of tectonic plates. When the plates push against each other, the rock where they meet is pushed upward, creating what are known as **fold mountains**. Most of the world's great mountain ranges, from the Himalayas to the Alps, were formed in this way.

These same forces can create a different type of mountain, called a **block mountain**, by working in exactly the opposite way. When tectonic plates move away

The movement of tectonic plates (outlined in red in this picture) help to form mountains.

from one another, enormous spaces, or **faults**, are created. Huge blocks of crust or strata move up, forming mountains, or down, creating valleys. This is how the Sierra Nevada, the mountain range that separates California and Nevada, was formed.

Some types of mountains are created by forces at work even deeper beneath the earth's surface. When hot, molten rock is forced to the surface, it may erupt violently, becoming **lava**. When the lava cools, it forms

California's San Andreas Fault is a line between two tectonic plates that are slowly moving away from each other.

19

a cone-shaped structure known as a **volcanic mountain**. Volcanic mountains are created very quickly compared with other types of mountains. Many of them remain active, which means they may erupt at any time.

Molten rock under the earth also creates another kind of mountain, very different from the volcano. Sometimes molten

Mount St. Helens, in Washington state, is an active volcano.

rock pushes upward, but does not force its way to the earth's surface. Instead, it pushes up a round, bulging formation of softer surface rock that surrounds it. The molten rock cools and hardens, and the softer rock around it eventually erodes, leaving behind a **dome mountain**. The Black Hills of South Dakota were formed in this way.

Mountains are rarely found alone. They are usually found as parts of mountain ranges that may extend for thousands of miles. Mountains in a range share common origins, such as being created at about the same time and by some of the same forces. Even with those things in common, a mountain range is not necessarily made up of just one type of mountain. The Andes, for example, are

The faces of four U.S. presidents have been carved into Mount Rushmore in the Black Hills mountains of South Dakota.

made up mostly of fold and block mountains, but have dozens of volcanic mountains as well.

The world's longest mountain ranges, however, mostly cannot be seen by human beings because they are deep underwater. The Mid-Atlantic Ridge, for example, runs more

The Andes mountain range is the longest found on land. It is almost 5,000 miles (8,000 km) long.

than 12,000 miles (19,312 km). That is almost the entire length of the North and South Atlantic oceans. Some experts believe the Mid-Atlantic

Ridge is part of an even larger undersea mountain range that covers 18,500 miles (29,773 km) across the Atlantic, Pacific, and Indian oceans. It is very difficult to be sure, however, because many of these undersea mountains have not yet been studied closely.

This photograph, taken by a satellite, shows the Himalayas as they appear from space.

Changing Mountains, Changing World

All mountains are very old, at least when compared to human beings and other living things. But some are far, far older than others. The highest mountains are usually among the youngest. The Himalayas, for example, began to form about 50 million years ago. The Appalachians of the eastern United States, by contrast, are at least 300 million years old. They are also much smaller than the Himalayas, and much smaller than they themselves once were. They have been worn down over time.

It may seem hard to believe, but mountains are actually changing all the time. Mount Everest is thought to be growing by about 1 inch (2.5 centimeters) every year.

The White Mountains, in New Hampshire, are part of the Appalachian mountain range.

The same forces that created the mountains, and are creating new ones, are also destroying them. This usually happens very slowly, over thousands or even millions of years. During this time, tectonic plates continue to shift, and volcanoes continue to erupt.

Mountains are changed by other forces, too, especially wind and water. These two forces cause **erosion**. Wind blows tiny rock particles against mountains, wearing them away. Rainwater freezes in the spaces between rocks and cracks them. And rivers flow down mountainsides, carrying rock and dirt that causes even more erosion. And **glaciers**, which are huge, slow-moving fields of ice, make deep cuts in even the hardest rock.

Mountains also affect the weather. When air strikes a mountain, for

The slow but powerful movements of glaciers make great changes in mountain formations.

example, it rises and becomes cooler. This makes the water droplets in the air form clouds that release rain or snow, which are essential for all life on Earth.

All life is closely connected with what happens to mountains. This is why we should all be concerned about what is happening to these landforms. **Global warming**, for example, is rapidly melting the snow and glaciers that have been found on mountain peaks for millions of years. If this trend continues, many parts of the world may find that they lack the water they need to support life. It is not an exaggeration to say that all life on Earth depends on mountains—and for this reason, we must take care to protect them.

Many different forms of life, such as these wildflowers, grow in mountainous regions.

Activity

CREATE YOUR OWN MOUNTAIN

Most of the world's mountains are fold mountains, which are created by horizontal pressure below the surface of the earth.

WHAT YOU WILL NEED

- several sheets of modeling clay (for example, Plasticine or Play-Doh brands) in different colors
- a table or other flat surface

WHAT TO DO

Place the sheets of modeling clay on the table, on top of each other, to represent the earth's strata. Then use your hands to press the sheets of clay together at the ends. The "strata" will rise up in folds in the middle, to create a fold mountain. The more clay you use, and the harder you press, the higher and steeper your mountain will be.

# Glossary

altitude—Height measured from a fixed point (for example, sea level).

base—The point where a mountain begins to rise from the surrounding land.

block mountain—A type of mountain (also known as a fault-block mountain) created when tectonic plates move apart, creating huge blocks of rock.

crust—The layer of the earth closest to the surface.

dome mountain—A type of mountain created when molten rock pushes upward but does not break through the earth's surface.

energy—Power.

erosion—The wearing away of landforms (for example, by wind or rain).

fault—An area between tectonic plates.

fold mountain—A type of mountain created when tectonic plates press together, forcing rock upward.

foothill—A smaller hill found around the base of the mountain.

geologist—A scientist who studies the structure of the earth.

geothermal energy—Heat produced naturally beneath the earth's surface.

glacier—A huge, slow-moving mass of ice.

global warming—The unusual increase in the earth's temperature in recent years.

landform—A naturally created feature on the earth's surface, such as a mountain or valley.

lava—Molten rock that reaches the earth's surface.

mountain range—A series of mountains, usually formed at about the same time and by the same set of natural forces.

peak—The highest point of a mountain (also called the summit).

sea level—The average level of the ocean's surface.

strata—The different layers of rock in the earth's crust.

tectonic plate—A huge, shifting slab of rock beneath the earth's surface.

timberline—The altitude on a mountain above which trees cannot grow.

valley—A low area at the base of the mountain.

volcanic mountain—A type of mountain created when molten rock pushes upward, breaks through the earth's surface, then cools and hardens.

# Find Out More

BOOKS

Anderson, Sheila. *Mountains*. New York: Lerner, 2007.

Bauer, Marion Dane. The Rocky Mountains (Ready-to-Read). New York: Aladdin, 2006.

Hynes, Margaret. *Mountains* (Kingfisher Young Knowledge). New York: Kingfisher Publications, 2007.

Levy, Janey. *Discovering Mountains* (World Habitats). New York: PowerKids Press, 2007.

WEB SITES

The Mountain Institute
http://www.mountain.org/education/explore.htm

World Mountain Encyclopedia
http://www.peakware.com/highest.html

All About Mount Kilimanjaro
http://www.pbs.org/wgbh/nova/kilimanjaro

Index

Page numbers in **boldface** are illustrations.